DISCOURSE
ON THE METHOD

OF RIGHTLY CONDUCTING THE REASON, AND SEEKING TRUTH IN THE SCIENCES

René Descartes

Translated by John Veitch

CLASSY
PUBLISHING

DISCOURSE ON THE METHOD
by René Descartes
Published by Classy Publishing, 2024

www.classypublishing.com
info@classypublishing.com

ISBN: 978-93-5522-433-0

CONTENTS

PREFATORY NOTE BY THE AUTHOR

If this Discourse appear too long to be read at once, it may be divided into six Parts: and, in the first, will be found various considerations touching the Sciences; in the second, the principal rules of the Method which the Author has discovered, in the third, certain of the rules of Morals which he has deduced from this Method; in the fourth, the reasonings by which he establishes the existence of God and of the Human Soul, which are the foundations of his Metaphysic; in the fifth, the order of the Physical questions which he has investigated, and, in particular, the explication of the motion of the heart and of some other difficulties pertaining to Medicine, as also the difference between the soul of man and that of the brutes; and, in the last, what the Author believes to be required in order to greater advancement in the investigation of Nature than has yet been made, with the reasons that have induced him to write.

PART I

Good sense is, of all things among men, the most equally distributed; for every one thinks himself so abundantly provided with it, that those even who are the most difficult to satisfy in everything else, do not usually desire a larger measure of this quality than they already possess. And in this it is not likely that all are mistaken the conviction is rather to be held as testifying that the power of judging aright and of distinguishing truth from error, which is properly what is called good sense or reason, is by nature equal in all men; and that the diversity of our opinions, consequently, does not arise from some being endowed with a larger share of reason than others, but solely from this, that we conduct our thoughts along different ways, and do not fix our attention on the same objects. For to be possessed of a vigorous mind is not enough; the prime requisite is rightly to apply it. The greatest minds, as they are capable of the highest excellences, are open likewise to the greatest aberrations; and those who travel very slowly may yet make far greater progress, provided they keep always to the straight road, than those who, while they run, forsake it.

For myself, I have never fancied my mind to be in any respect more perfect than those of the generality; on the contrary, I have often wished that I were equal to some others in promptitude of thought, or in clearness and distinctness of imagination, or in fullness and readiness of memory. And besides these, I know of no other qualities that contribute to the perfection of the mind; for as to the reason or sense, inasmuch as it is that alone which constitutes us men, and distinguishes us from the brutes, I am disposed to believe that it is to be found complete in each individual; and on this point to adopt the common opinion of philosophers, who say that the difference of greater and less holds only among the accidents, and not among the forms or natures of individuals of the same species.

I will not hesitate, however, to avow my belief that it has been my singular good fortune to have very early in life fallen in with certain tracks which have conducted me to considerations and maxims, of which I have formed a method that gives me the means, as I think, of gradually augmenting my knowledge, and of raising it by little and little to the highest point which the mediocrity of my talents and the brief duration of my life will permit me to reach. For I have already reaped from it such fruits that, although I have been accustomed to think lowly enough of myself, and although when I look with the eye of a philosopher at the varied courses and pursuits of mankind at large, I find scarcely one which does not appear in vain and useless, I nevertheless derive the highest satisfaction from the progress I conceive myself to have already made in the search after truth, and cannot help entertaining such expectations of the future as to believe that if, among the occupations of men as men, there is any one really excellent and important, it is that which I have chosen.

After all, it is possible I may be mistaken; and it is but a little copper and glass, perhaps, that I take for gold and diamonds. I know how very liable we are to delusion in what relates to ourselves, and also how much the judgments of our friends are to be suspected when given in our favor. But I shall endeavor in this discourse to describe the paths I have followed, and to delineate my life as in a picture, in order that each one may also be able to judge of them for himself, and that in the general opinion entertained of them, as gathered from current report, I myself may have a new help towards instruction to be added to those I have been in the habit of employing.

My present design, then, is not to teach the method which each ought to follow for the right conduct of his reason, but solely to describe the way in which I have endeavored to conduct my own. They who set themselves to give precepts must of course regard themselves as possessed of greater skill than those to whom they prescribe; and if they err in the slightest particular, they subject themselves to censure. But as this tract is put forth merely as a history, or, if you will, as a tale, in which, amid some examples worthy of imitation, there will be found, perhaps, as many more which it were advisable not to follow, I hope it will prove useful to some without being hurtful to any, and that my openness will find some favor with all.

From my childhood, I have been familiar with letters; and as I was given to believe that by their help a clear and certain knowledge of all that is useful in life might be acquired, I was ardently desirous of instruction. But as soon as I had finished the entire course of study, at the close of which it is customary to be admitted into the order of the learned, I completely changed my opinion. For I found myself involved in so many doubts and errors, that I was convinced I had advanced no farther in all my attempts at learning, than the discovery at every turn of my own ignorance. And yet I was studying in one of the most celebrated schools in Europe, in which I thought there must be learned men, if such were anywhere to be found. I had been taught all that others learned there; and not contented with the sciences actually taught us, I had, in addition, read all the books that had fallen into my hands, treating of such branches as are esteemed the most curious and rare. I knew the judgment which others had formed of me; and I did not find that I was considered inferior to my fellows, although there were among them some who were already marked out to fill the places of our instructors. And, in fine, our age appeared to me as flourishing, and as fertile in powerful minds as any preceding one. I was thus led to take the liberty of judging of all other men by myself, and of concluding that there was no science in existence that was of such a nature as I had previously been given to believe.

I still continued, however, to hold in esteem the studies of the schools. I was aware that the languages taught in them are necessary to the understanding of the writings of the ancients; that the grace of fable stirs the mind; that the memorable deeds of history elevate it; and, if read with discretion, aid in forming the judgment; that the perusal of all excellent books is, as it were, to interview with the noblest men of past ages, who have written them, and even a studied interview, in which are discovered to us only their choicest thoughts; that eloquence has incomparable force and beauty; that poesy has its ravishing graces and delights; that in the mathematics there are many refined discoveries eminently suited to gratify the inquisitive, as well as further all the arts an lessen the labour of man; that numerous highly useful precepts and exhortations to virtue are contained in treatises on morals; that theology points out the path to heaven; that philosophy affords the means of discoursing with an appearance of truth on all matters, and commands the admiration of the more simple; that jurisprudence, medicine, and the other sciences, secure for their cultivators honors and riches; and, in fine, that it is useful to bestow some attention upon all, even upon those abounding the most in superstition and error, that we may be in a position to determine their real value, and guard against being deceived.

But I believed that I had already given sufficient time to languages, and likewise to the reading of the writings of the ancients, to their histories and fables. For to hold converse with those of other ages and to travel, are almost the same thing. It is useful to know something of the manners of different nations, that we may be enabled to form a more correct judgment regarding our own, and be prevented from thinking that everything contrary to our customs is ridiculous and irrational, a conclusion usually come to by those whose experience has been limited to their own country. On the other hand, when too much time is occupied in traveling, we become strangers to our native country; and the over curious in the customs of the past are generally ignorant of those of the present. Besides, fictitious narratives lead us to imagine the possibility of many events that are impossible; and even the most faithful histories, if they do not wholly misrepresent matters, or exaggerate their importance to render the account of them more worthy of perusal, omit, at least, almost always the meanest and least striking of the attendant circumstances; hence it happens that the remainder does not represent the truth, and that such as regulate their conduct by examples drawn from this source, are apt to fall into the extravagances of the knight-errants of romance, and to entertain projects that exceed their powers.

I esteemed eloquence highly, and was in raptures with poesy; but I thought that both were gifts of nature rather than fruits of study. Those in whom the faculty of reason is predominant, and who most skillfully dispose their thoughts with a view to render them clear and intelligible, are always the best able to persuade others of the truth of what they lay down, though they should speak only in the language of Lower Brittany, and be wholly ignorant of the rules of rhetoric; and those whose minds are stored with the most agreeable fancies, and who can give expression to them with the greatest embellishment and harmony, are still the best poets, though unacquainted with the art of poetry.

I was especially delighted with the mathematics, on account of the certitude and evidence of their reasonings; but I had not as yet a precise knowledge of their true use; and thinking that they but contributed to the advancement of the mechanical arts, I was astonished that foundations, so strong and solid, should have had no loftier superstructure reared on them. On the other hand, I compared the disquisitions of the ancient moralists to very towering and magnificent palaces with no better foundation than sand and mud: they laud the virtues very highly, and exhibit them as estimable far above anything on earth; but they give us no adequate criterion of virtue, and frequently that which they designate with so fine a name is but apathy, or pride, or despair, or parricide.

I revered our theology, and aspired as much as any one to reach heaven: but being given assuredly to understand that the way is not less open to the most ignorant than to the most learned, and that the revealed truths which lead to heaven are above our comprehension, I did not presume to subject them to the impotency of my reason; and I thought that in order competently to undertake their examination, there was need of some special help from heaven, and of being more than man.

Of philosophy I will say nothing, except that when I saw that it had been cultivated for many ages by the most distinguished men, and that yet there is not a single matter within its sphere which is not still in dispute, and nothing, therefore, which is above doubt, I did not presume to anticipate that my success would be greater in it than that of others; and further, when I considered the number of conflicting opinions touching a single matter that may be upheld by learned men, while there can be but one true, I reckoned as well-nigh false all that was only probable.

As to the other sciences, inasmuch as these borrow their principles from philosophy, I judged that no solid superstructures could be reared on foundations so infirm; and neither the honor nor the gain held out by them was sufficient to determine me to their cultivation: for I was not, thank Heaven, in a condition which compelled me to make merchandise of science for the bettering of my fortune; and though I might not profess to scorn glory as a cynic, I yet made very slight account of that honor which I hoped to acquire only through fictitious titles. And, in fine, of false sciences I thought I knew the worth sufficiently to escape being deceived by the professions of an alchemist, the predictions of an astrologer, the impostures of a magician, or by the artifices and boasting of any of those who profess to know things of which they are ignorant.

For these reasons, as soon as my age permitted me to pass from under the control of my instructors, I entirely abandoned the study of letters, and resolved no longer to seek any other science than the knowledge of myself, or of the great book of the world. I spent the remainder of my youth in traveling, in visiting courts and armies, in holding intercourse with men of different dispositions and ranks, in collecting varied experience, in proving myself in the different situations into which fortune threw me, and, above all, in making such reflection on the matter of my experience as to secure my improvement. For it occurred to me that I should find much more truth in the reasonings of each individual with reference to the affairs in which he is personally interested, and the issue of which must presently punish him if he has judged amiss, than in those conducted by a man of letters in his study, regarding speculative matters that are of no practical moment, and followed by no consequences to himself, farther, perhaps, than that they foster his vanity the better the more remote they are from common sense; requiring, as they must in this case, the exercise of greater ingenuity and art to render them probable. In addition, I had always a most earnest desire to know how to distinguish the true from the false, in order that I might be able clearly to discriminate the right path in life, and proceed in it with confidence.

It is true that, while busied only in considering the manners of other men, I found here, too, scarce any ground for settled conviction, and remarked hardly less contradiction among them than in the opinions of the philosophers. So that the greatest advantage I derived from the study consisted in this, that, observing many things which, however extravagant and ridiculous to our apprehension, are yet by common consent received and approved by other great nations, I learned to entertain too decided a belief in regard to nothing of the truth of which I had been persuaded merely by example and custom; and thus I gradually extricated myself from many errors powerful enough to darken our natural intelligence, and incapacitate us in great measure from listening to reason. But after I had been occupied several years in thus studying the book of the world, and in essaying to gather some experience, I at length resolved to make myself an object of study, and to employ all the powers of my mind in choosing the paths I ought to follow, an undertaking which was accompanied with greater success than it would have been had I never quitted my country or my books.

PART II

I was then in Germany, attracted thither by the wars in that country, which have not yet been brought to a termination; and as I was returning to the army from the coronation of the emperor, the setting in of winter arrested me in a locality where, as I found no society to interest me, and was besides fortunately undisturbed by any cares or passions, I remained the whole day in seclusion, with full opportunity to occupy my attention with my own thoughts. Of these one of the very first that occurred to me was, that there is seldom so much perfection in works composed of many separate parts, upon which different hands had been employed, as in those completed by a single master. Thus it is observable that the buildings which a single architect has planned and executed, are generally more elegant and commodious than those which several have attempted to improve, by making old walls serve for purposes for which they were not originally built. Thus also, those ancient cities which, from being at first only villages, have become, in course of time, large towns, are usually but ill laid out compared with the regularity constructed towns which a professional architect has freely planned on an open plain; so that although the several buildings of the former may often equal or surpass in beauty those of the latter, yet when one observes their indiscriminate juxtaposition, there a large one and here a small, and the consequent crookedness and irregularity of the streets, one is disposed to allege that chance rather than any human will guided by reason must have led to such an arrangement. And if we consider that nevertheless there have been at all times certain officers whose duty it was to see that private buildings contributed to public ornament, the difficulty of reaching high perfection with but the materials of others to operate on, will be readily acknowledged. In the same way I fancied that those nations which, starting from a semi-barbarous state and advancing to civilization by slow degrees, have had their laws successively determined, and, as it were, forced upon them simply by experience of the hurtfulness of particular crimes and disputes, would by this process come to be possessed of less perfect institutions than those which, from the commencement of their association as communities, have followed the appointments of some wise legislator. It is thus quite certain that the constitution of the true religion, the ordinances of which are derived from God, must be incomparably superior to that of every other. And, to speak of human affairs, I believe that the pre-eminence of Sparta was due not to the goodness of each of its laws in particular, for many of these were very strange, and even opposed to good morals, but to the circumstance that, originated by a single individual, they all tended to a single end. In the same way I thought that the sciences contained in books (such of them at least as are made up of probable reasonings, without demonstrations), composed as they are of the opinions of many different individuals massed together, are farther removed from truth than the simple inferences which a man of good sense using his natural and unprejudiced judgment draws respecting the matters of his experience. And because we have all to pass through a state of infancy to manhood, and have been of necessity, for a length of time, governed by our desires and preceptors (whose dictates were frequently conflicting, while neither perhaps always counseled us for the best), I farther concluded that it is almost impossible that our judgments can be so correct or solid as they would have been, had our reason been mature from the moment of our birth, and had we always been guided by it alone.

It is true, however, that it is not customary to pull down all the houses of a town with the single design of rebuilding them differently, and thereby rendering the streets more handsome; but it often happens that a private individual takes down his own with the view of erecting it anew, and that people are even sometimes constrained to this when their houses are in danger of falling from age, or when the foundations are insecure. With this before me by way of example, I was persuaded that it would indeed be preposterous for a private individual to think of reforming a state by fundamentally changing it throughout, and overturning it in order to set it up amended; and the same I thought was true of any similar project for reforming the body of the sciences, or the order of teaching them established in the schools: but as for the opinions which up to that time I had embraced, I thought that I could not do better than resolve at once to sweep them wholly away, that I might afterwards be in a position to admit either others more correct, or even perhaps the same when they had undergone the scrutiny of reason. I firmly believed that in this way I should much better succeed in the conduct of my life, than if I built only upon old foundations, and leaned upon principles which, in my youth, I had taken upon trust. For although I recognized various difficulties in this undertaking, these were not, however, without remedy, nor once to be compared with such as attend the slightest reformation in public affairs. Large bodies, if once overthrown, are with great difficulty set up again, or even kept erect when once seriously shaken, and the fall of such is always disastrous. Then if there are any imperfections in the constitutions of states (and that many such exist the diversity of constitutions is alone sufficient to assure us), custom has without doubt materially smoothed their inconveniences, and has even managed to steer altogether clear of, or insensibly corrected a number which sagacity could not have provided against with equal effect; and, in fine, the defects are almost always more tolerable than the change necessary for their removal; in the same manner that highways which wind among mountains, by being much frequented, become gradually so smooth and commodious, that it is much better to follow them than to seek a straighter path by climbing over the tops of rocks and descending to the bottoms of precipices.

Hence it is that I cannot in any degree approve of those restless and busy meddlers who, called neither by birth nor fortune to take part in the management of public affairs, are yet always projecting reforms; and if I thought that this tract contained aught which might justify the suspicion that I was a victim of such folly, I would by no means permit its publication. I have never contemplated anything higher than the reformation of my own opinions, and basing them on a foundation wholly my own. And although my own satisfaction with my work has led me to present here a draft of it, I do not by any means therefore recommend to every one else to make a similar attempt. Those whom God has endowed with a larger measure of genius will entertain, perhaps, designs still more exalted; but for the many I am much afraid lest even the present undertaking be more than they can safely venture to imitate. The single design to strip one's self of all past beliefs is one that ought not to be taken by every one. The majority of men is composed of two classes, for neither of which would this be at all a befitting resolution: in the first place, of those who with more than a due confidence in their own powers, are precipitate in their judgments and want the patience requisite for orderly and circumspect thinking; whence it happens, that if men of this class once take the liberty to doubt of their accustomed opinions, and quit the beaten highway, they will never be able to thread the byway that would lead them by a shorter course, and will lose themselves and continue to wander for life; in the second place, of those who, possessed of sufficient sense or modesty to determine that there are others who excel them in the power of discriminating between truth and error, and by whom they may be instructed, ought rather to content themselves with the opinions of such than trust for more correct to their own reason.

For my own part, I should doubtless have belonged to the latter class, had I received instruction from but one master, or had I never known the diversities of opinion that from time immemorial have prevailed among men of the greatest learning. But I had become aware, even so early as during my college life, that no opinion, however absurd and incredible, can be imagined, which has not been maintained by some on of the philosophers; and afterwards in the course of my travels I remarked that all those whose opinions are decidedly repugnant to ours are not in that account barbarians and savages, but on the contrary that many of these nations make an equally good, if not better, use of their reason than we do. I took into account also the very different character which a person brought up from infancy in France or Germany exhibits, from that which, with the same mind originally, this individual would have possessed had he lived always among the Chinese or with savages, and the circumstance that in dress itself the fashion which pleased us ten years ago, and which may again, perhaps, be received into favor before ten years have gone, appears to us at this moment extravagant and ridiculous. I was thus led to infer that the ground of our opinions is far more custom and example than any certain knowledge. And, finally, although such be the ground of our opinions, I remarked that a plurality of suffrages is no guarantee of truth where it is at all of difficult discovery, as in such cases it is much more likely that it will be found by one than by many. I could, however, select from the crowd no one whose opinions seemed worthy of preference, and thus I found myself constrained, as it were, to use my own reason in the conduct of my life.

But like one walking alone and in the dark, I resolved to proceed so slowly and with such circumspection, that if I did not advance far, I would at least guard against falling. I did not even choose to dismiss summarily any of the opinions that had crept into my belief without having been introduced by reason, but first of all took sufficient time carefully to satisfy myself of the general nature of the task I was setting myself, and ascertain the true method by which to arrive at the knowledge of whatever lay within the compass of my powers.

Among the branches of philosophy, I had, at an earlier period, given some attention to logic, and among those of the mathematics to geometrical analysis and algebra,—three arts or sciences which ought, as I conceived, to contribute something to my design. But, on examination, I found that, as for logic, its syllogisms and the majority of its other precepts are of avail—rather in the communication of what we already know, or even as the art of Lully, in speaking without judgment of things of which we are ignorant, than in the investigation of the unknown; and although this science contains indeed a number of correct and very excellent precepts, there are, nevertheless, so many others, and these either injurious or superfluous, mingled with the former, that it is almost quite as difficult to effect a severance of the true from the false as it is to extract a Diana or a Minerva from a rough block of marble. Then as to the analysis of the ancients and the algebra of the moderns, besides that they embrace only matters highly abstract, and, to appearance, of no use, the former is so exclusively restricted to the consideration of figures, that it can exercise the understanding only on condition of greatly fatiguing the imagination; and, in the latter, there is so complete a subjection to certain rules and formulas, that there results an art full of confusion and obscurity calculated to embarrass, instead of a science fitted to cultivate the mind. By these considerations I was induced to seek some other method which would comprise the advantages of the three and be exempt from their defects. And as a multitude of laws often only hampers justice, so that a state is best governed when, with few laws, these are rigidly administered; in like manner, instead of the great number of precepts of which logic is composed, I believed that the four following would prove perfectly sufficient for me, provided I took the firm and unwavering resolution never in a single instance to fail in observing them.

The first was never to accept anything for true which I did not clearly know to be such; that is to say, carefully to avoid precipitancy and prejudice, and to comprise nothing more in my judgement than what was presented to my mind so clearly and distinctly as to exclude all ground of doubt.

The second, to divide each of the difficulties under examination into as many parts as possible, and as might be necessary for its adequate solution.

The third, to conduct my thoughts in such order that, by commencing with objects the simplest and easiest to know, I might ascend by little and little, and, as it were, step by step, to the knowledge of the more complex; assigning in thought a certain order even to those objects which in their own nature do not stand in a relation of antecedence and sequence.

And the *last*, in every case to make enumerations so complete, and reviews so general, that I might be assured that nothing was omitted.

The long chains of simple and easy reasonings by means of which geometers are accustomed to reach the conclusions of their most difficult demonstrations, had led me to imagine that all things, to the knowledge of which man is competent, are mutually connected in the same way, and that there is nothing so far removed from us as to be beyond our reach, or so hidden that we cannot discover it, provided only we abstain from accepting the false for the true, and always preserve in our thoughts the order necessary for the deduction of one truth from another. And I had little difficulty in determining the objects with which it was necessary to commence, for I was already persuaded that it must be with the simplest and easiest to know, and, considering that of all those who have hitherto sought truth in the sciences, the mathematicians alone have been able to find any demonstrations, that is, any certain and evident reasons, I did not doubt but that such must have been the rule of their investigations. I resolved to commence, therefore, with the examination of the simplest objects, not anticipating, however, from this any other advantage than that to be found in accustoming my mind to the love and nourishment of truth, and to a distaste for all such reasonings as were unsound. But I had no intention on that account of attempting to master all the particular sciences commonly denominated mathematics: but observing that, however different their objects, they all agree in considering only the various relations or proportions subsisting among those objects, I thought it best for my purpose to consider these proportions in the most general form possible, without referring them to any objects in particular, except such as would most facilitate the knowledge of them, and without by any means restricting them to these, that afterwards I might thus be the better able to apply them to every other class of objects to which they are legitimately applicable. Perceiving further, that in order to understand these relations I should sometimes have to consider them one by one and sometimes only to bear them in mind, or embrace them in the aggregate, I thought that, in order the better to consider them individually, I should view them as subsisting between straight lines, than which I could find no objects more simple, or capable of being more distinctly represented to my imagination and senses; and on the other hand, that in order to retain them in the memory or embrace an aggregate of many, I should express them by certain characters the briefest possible. In this way I believed that I could borrow all that was best both in geometrical analysis and in algebra, and correct all the defects of the one by help of the other.

And, in point of fact, the accurate observance of these few precepts gave me, I take the liberty of saying, such ease in unraveling all the questions embraced in these two sciences, that in the two or three months I devoted to their examination, not only did I reach solutions of questions I had formerly deemed exceedingly difficult but even as regards questions of the solution of which I continued ignorant, I was enabled, as it appeared to me, to determine the means whereby, and the extent to which a solution was possible; results attributable to the circumstance that I commenced with the simplest and most general truths, and that thus each truth discovered was a rule available in the discovery of subsequent ones Nor in this perhaps shall I appear too vain, if it be considered that, as the truth on any particular point is one whoever apprehends the truth, knows all that on that point can be known. The child, for example, who has been instructed in the elements of arithmetic, and has made a particular addition, according to rule, may be assured that he has found, with respect to the sum of the numbers before him, and that in this instance is within the reach of human genius. Now, in conclusion, the method which teaches adherence to the true order, and an exact enumeration of all the conditions of the thing sought includes all that gives certitude to the rules of arithmetic.

But the chief ground of my satisfaction with thus method, was the assurance I had of thereby exercising my reason in all matters, if not with absolute perfection, at least with the greatest attainable by me: besides, I was conscious that by its use my mind was becoming gradually habituated to clearer and more distinct conceptions of its objects; and I hoped also, from not having restricted this method to any particular matter, to apply it to the difficulties of the other sciences, with not less success than to those of algebra. I should not, however, on this account have ventured at once on the examination of all the difficulties of the sciences which presented themselves to me, for this would have been contrary to the order prescribed in the method, but observing that the knowledge of such is dependent on principles borrowed from philosophy, in which I found nothing certain, I thought it necessary first of all to endeavor to establish its principles. And because I observed, besides, that an inquiry of this kind was of all others of the greatest moment, and one in which precipitancy and anticipation in judgment were most to be dreaded, I thought that I ought not to approach it till I had reached a more mature age (being at that time but twenty-three), and had first of all employed much of my time in preparation for the work, as well by eradicating from my mind all the erroneous opinions I had up to that moment accepted, as by amassing variety of experience to afford materials for my reasonings, and by continually exercising myself in my chosen method with a view to increased skill in its application.

PART III

And finally, as it is not enough, before commencing to rebuild the house in which we live, that it be pulled down, and materials and builders provided, or that we engage in the work ourselves, according to a plan which we have beforehand carefully drawn out, but as it is likewise necessary that we be furnished with some other house in which we may live commodiously during the operations, so that I might not remain irresolute in my actions, while my reason compelled me to suspend my judgement, and that I might not be prevented from living thenceforward in the greatest possible felicity, I formed a provisory code of morals, composed of three or four maxims, with which I am desirous to make you acquainted.

The *first* was to obey the laws and customs of my country, adhering firmly to the faith in which, by the grace of God, I had been educated from my childhood and regulating my conduct in every other matter according to the most moderate opinions, and the farthest removed from extremes, which should happen to be adopted in practice with general consent of the most judicious of those among whom I might be living. For as I had from that time begun to hold my own opinions for nought because I wished to subject them all to examination, I was convinced that I could not do better than follow in the meantime the opinions of the most judicious; and although there are some perhaps among the Persians and Chinese as judicious as among ourselves, expediency seemed to dictate that I should regulate my practice conformably to the opinions of those with whom I should have to live; and it appeared to me that, in order to ascertain the real opinions of such, I ought rather to take cognizance of what they practised than of what they said, not only because, in the corruption of our manners, there are few disposed to speak exactly as they believe, but also because very many are not aware of what it is that they really believe; for, as the act of mind by which a thing is believed is different from that by which we know that we believe it, the one act is often found without the other. Also, amid many opinions held in equal repute, I chose always the most moderate, as much for the reason that these are always the most convenient for practice, and probably the best (for all excess is generally vicious), as that, in the event of my falling into error, I might be at less distance from the truth than if, having chosen one of the extremes, it should turn out to be the other which I ought to have adopted. And I placed in the class of extremes especially all promises by which somewhat of our freedom is abridged; not that I disapproved of the laws which, to provide against the instability of men of feeble resolution, when what is sought to be accomplished is some good, permit engagements by vows and contracts binding the parties to persevere in it, or even, for the security of commerce, sanction similar engagements where the purpose sought to be realized is indifferent: but because I did not find anything on earth which was wholly superior to change, and because, for myself in particular, I hoped gradually to perfect my judgments, and not to suffer them to deteriorate, I would have deemed it a grave sin against good sense, if, for the reason that I approved of something at a particular time, I therefore bound myself to hold it for good at a subsequent time, when perhaps it had ceased to be so, or I had ceased to esteem it such.

My *second* maxim was to be as firm and resolute in my actions as I was able, and not to adhere less steadfastly to the most doubtful opinions, when once adopted, than if they had been highly certain; imitating in this the example of travelers who, when they have lost their way in a forest, ought not to wander from side to side, far less remain in one place, but proceed constantly towards the same side in as straight a line as possible, without changing their direction for slight reasons, although perhaps it might be chance alone which at first determined the selection; for in this way, if they do not exactly reach the point they desire, they will come at least in the end to some place that will probably be preferable to the middle of a forest. In the same way, since in action it frequently happens that no delay is permissible, it is very certain that, when it is not in our power to determine what is true, we ought to act according to what is most probable; and even although we should not remark a greater probability in one opinion than in another, we ought notwithstanding to choose one or the other, and afterwards consider it, in so far as it relates to practice, as no longer dubious, but manifestly true and certain, since the reason by which our choice has been determined is itself possessed of these qualities. This principle was sufficient thenceforward to rid me of all those repentings and pangs of remorse that usually disturb the consciences of such feeble and uncertain minds as, destitute of any clear and determinate principle of choice, allow themselves one day to adopt a course of action as the best, which they abandon the next, as the opposite.

My *third* maxim was to endeavor always to conquer myself rather than fortune, and change my desires rather than the order of the world, and in general, accustom myself to the persuasion that, except our own thoughts, there is nothing absolutely in our power; so that when we have done our best in things external to us, all wherein we fail of success is to be held, as regards us, absolutely impossible: and this single principle seemed to me sufficient to prevent me from desiring for the future anything which I could not obtain, and thus render me contented; for since our will naturally seeks those objects alone which the understanding represents as in some way possible of attainment, it is plain, that if we consider all external goods as equally beyond our power, we shall no more regret the absence of such goods as seem due to our birth, when deprived of them without any fault of ours, than our not possessing the kingdoms of China or Mexico, and thus making, so to speak, a virtue of necessity, we shall no more desire health in disease, or freedom in imprisonment, than we now do bodies incorruptible as diamonds, or the wings of birds to fly with. But I confess there is need of prolonged discipline and frequently repeated meditation to accustom the mind to view all objects in this light; and I believe that in this chiefly consisted the secret of the power of such philosophers as in former times were enabled to rise superior to the influence of fortune, and, amid suffering and poverty, enjoy a happiness which their gods might have envied. For, occupied incessantly with the consideration of the limits prescribed to their power by nature, they became so entirely convinced that nothing was at their disposal except their own thoughts, that this conviction was of itself sufficient to prevent their entertaining any desire of other objects; and over their thoughts they acquired a sway so absolute, that they had some ground on this account for esteeming themselves more rich and more powerful, more free and more happy, than other men who, whatever be the favors heaped on them by nature and fortune, if destitute of this philosophy, can never command the realization of all their desires.

In fine, to conclude this code of morals, I thought of reviewing the different occupations of men in this life, with the view of making choice of the best. And, without wishing to offer any remarks on the employments of others, I may state that it was my conviction that I could not do better than continue in that in which I was engaged, viz., in devoting my whole life to the culture of my reason, and in making the greatest progress I was able in the knowledge of truth, on the principles of the method which I had prescribed to myself. This method, from the time I had begun to apply it, had been to me the source of satisfaction so intense as to lead me to, believe that more perfect or more innocent could not be enjoyed in this life; and as by its means I daily discovered truths that appeared to me of some importance, and of which other men were generally ignorant, the gratification thence arising so occupied my mind that I was wholly indifferent to every other object. Besides, the three preceding maxims were founded singly on the design of continuing the work of self-instruction. For since God has endowed each of us with some light of reason by which to distinguish truth from error, I could not have believed that I ought for a single moment to rest satisfied with the opinions of another, unless I had resolved to exercise my own judgment in examining these whenever I should be duly qualified for the task. Nor could I have proceeded on such opinions without scruple, had I supposed that I should thereby forfeit any advantage for attaining still more accurate, should such exist. And, in fine, I could not have restrained my desires, nor remained satisfied had I not followed a path in which I thought myself certain of attaining all the knowledge to the acquisition of which I was competent, as well as the largest amount of what is truly good which I could ever hope to secure

Inasmuch as we neither seek nor shun any object except in so far as our understanding represents it as good or bad, all that is necessary to right action is right judgment, and to the best action the most correct judgment, that is, to the acquisition of all the virtues with all else that is truly valuable and within our reach; and the assurance of such an acquisition cannot fail to render us contented.

Having thus provided myself with these maxims, and having placed them in reserve along with the truths of faith, which have ever occupied the first place in my belief, I came to the conclusion that I might with freedom set about ridding myself of what remained of my opinions. And, inasmuch as I hoped to be better able successfully to accomplish this work by holding intercourse with mankind, than by remaining longer shut up in the retirement where these thoughts had occurred to me, I betook me again to traveling before the winter was well ended. And, during the nine subsequent years, I did nothing but roam from one place to another, desirous of being a spectator rather than an actor in the plays exhibited on the theater of the world; and, as I made it my business in each matter to reflect particularly upon what might fairly be doubted and prove a source of error, I gradually rooted out from my mind all the errors which had hitherto crept into it. Not that in this I imitated the sceptics who doubt only that they may doubt, and seek nothing beyond uncertainty itself; for, on the contrary, my design was singly to find ground of assurance, and cast aside the loose earth and sand, that I might reach the rock or the clay. In this, as appears to me, I was successful enough; for, since I endeavored to discover the falsehood or incertitude of the propositions I examined, not by feeble conjectures, but by clear and certain reasonings, I met with nothing so doubtful as not to yield some conclusion of adequate certainty, although this were merely the inference, that the matter in question contained nothing certain. And, just as in pulling down an old house, we usually reserve the ruins to contribute towards the erection, so, in destroying such of my opinions as I judged to be Ill-founded, I made a variety of observations and acquired an amount of experience of which I availed myself in the establishment of more certain. And further, I continued to exercise myself in the method I had prescribed; for, besides taking care in general to conduct all my thoughts according to its rules, I reserved some hours from time to time which I expressly devoted to the employment of the method in the solution of mathematical difficulties, or even in the solution likewise of some questions belonging to other sciences, but which, by my having detached them from such principles of these sciences as were of inadequate certainty, were rendered almost mathematical: the truth of this will be manifest from the numerous examples contained in this volume. And thus, without in appearance living otherwise than those who, with no other occupation than that of spending their lives agreeably and innocently, study to sever pleasure from vice, and who, that they may enjoy their leisure without ennui, have recourse to such pursuits as are honorable, I was nevertheless prosecuting my design, and making greater progress in the knowledge of truth, than I might, perhaps, have made had I been engaged in the perusal of books merely, or in holding converse with men of letters.

These nine years passed away, however, before I had come to any determinate judgment respecting the difficulties which form matter of dispute among the learned, or had commenced to seek the principles of any philosophy more certain than the vulgar. And the examples of many men of the highest genius, who had, in former times, engaged in this inquiry, but, as appeared to me, without success, led me to imagine it to be a work of so much difficulty, that I would not perhaps have ventured on it so soon had I not heard it currently rumored that I had already completed the inquiry. I know not what were the grounds of this opinion; and, if my conversation contributed in any measure to its rise, this must have happened rather from my having confessed my Ignorance with greater freedom than those are accustomed to do who have studied a little, and expounded perhaps, the reasons that led me to doubt of many of those things that by others are esteemed certain, than from my having boasted of any system of philosophy. But, as I am of a disposition that makes me unwilling to be esteemed different from what I really am, I thought it necessary to endeavor by all means to render myself worthy of the reputation accorded to me; and it is now exactly eight years since this desire constrained me to remove from all those places where interruption from any of my acquaintances was possible, and betake myself to this country, in which the long duration of the war has led to the establishment of such discipline, that the armies maintained seem to be of use only in enabling the inhabitants to enjoy more securely the blessings of peace and where, in the midst of a great crowd actively engaged in business, and more careful of their own affairs than curious about those of others, I have been enabled to live without being deprived of any of the conveniences to be had in the most populous cities, and yet as solitary and as retired as in the midst of the most remote deserts.

PART IV

I am in doubt as to the propriety of making my first meditations in the place above mentioned matter of discourse; for these are so metaphysical, and so uncommon, as not, perhaps, to be acceptable to every one. And yet, that it may be determined whether the foundations that I have laid are sufficiently secure, I find myself in a measure constrained to advert to them. I had long before remarked that, in relation to practice, it is sometimes necessary to adopt, as if above doubt, opinions which we discern to be highly uncertain, as has been already said; but as I then desired to give my attention solely to the search after truth, I thought that a procedure exactly the opposite was called for, and that I ought to reject as absolutely false all opinions in regard to which I could suppose the least ground for doubt, in order to ascertain whether after that there remained aught in my belief that was wholly indubitable. Accordingly, seeing that our senses sometimes deceive us, I was willing to suppose that there existed nothing really such as they presented to us; and because some men err in reasoning, and fall into paralogisms, even on the simplest matters of geometry, I, convinced that I was as open to error as any other, rejected as false all the reasonings I had hitherto taken for demonstrations; and finally, when I considered that the very same thoughts (presentations) which we experience when awake may also be experienced when we are asleep, while there is at that time not one of them true, I supposed that all the objects (presentations) that had ever entered into my mind when awake, had in them no more truth than the illusions of my dreams. But immediately upon this I observed that, whilst I thus wished to think that all was false, it was absolutely necessary that I, who thus thought, should be somewhat; and as I observed that this truth, I think, therefore I am (COGITO ERGO SUM), was so certain and of such evidence that no ground of doubt, however extravagant, could be alleged by the sceptics capable of shaking it, I concluded that I might, without scruple, accept it as the first principle of the philosophy of which I was in search.

In the next place, I attentively examined what I was and as I observed that I could suppose that I had no body, and that there was no world nor any place in which I might be; but that I could not therefore suppose that I was not; and that, on the contrary, from the very circumstance that I thought to doubt of the truth of other things, it most clearly and certainly followed that I was; while, on the other hand, if I had only ceased to think, although all the other objects which I had ever imagined had been in reality existent, I would have had no reason to believe that I existed; I thence concluded that I was a substance whose whole essence or nature consists only in thinking, and which, that it may exist, has need of no place, nor is dependent on any material thing; so that "I," that is to say, the mind by which I am what I am, is wholly distinct from the body, and is even more easily known than the latter, and is such, that although the latter were not, it would still continue to be all that it is.

After this I inquired in general into what is essential to the truth and certainty of a proposition; for since I had discovered one which I knew to be true, I thought that I must likewise be able to discover the ground of this certitude. And as I observed that in the words I think, therefore I am, there is nothing at all which gives me assurance of their truth beyond this, that I see very clearly that in order to think it is necessary to exist, I concluded that I might take, as a general rule, the principle, that all the things which we very clearly and distinctly conceive are true, only observing, however, that there is some difficulty in rightly determining the objects which we distinctly conceive.

In the next place, from reflecting on the circumstance that I doubted, and that consequently my being was not wholly perfect (for I clearly saw that it was a greater perfection to know than to doubt), I was led to inquire whence I had learned to think of something more perfect than myself; and I clearly recognized that I must hold this notion from some nature which in reality was more perfect. As for the thoughts of many other objects external to me, as of the sky, the earth, light, heat, and a thousand more, I was less at a loss to know whence these came; for since I remarked in them nothing which seemed to render them superior to myself, I could believe that, if these were true, they were dependencies on my own nature, in so far as it possessed a certain perfection, and, if they were false, that I held them from nothing, that is to say, that they were in me because of a certain imperfection of my nature. But this could not be the case with-the idea of a nature more perfect than myself; for to receive it from nothing was a thing manifestly impossible; and, because it is not less repugnant that the more perfect should be an effect of, and dependence on the less perfect, than that something should proceed from nothing, it was equally impossible that I could hold it from myself: accordingly, it but remained that it had been placed in me by a nature which was in reality more perfect than mine, and which even possessed within itself all the perfections of which I could form any idea; that is to say, in a single word, which was God. And to this I added that, since I knew some perfections which I did not possess, I was not the only being in existence (I will here, with your permission, freely use the terms of the schools); but, on the contrary, that there was of necessity some other more perfect Being upon whom I was dependent, and from whom I had received all that I possessed; for if I had existed alone, and independently of every other being, so as to have had from myself all the perfection, however little, which I actually possessed, I should have been able, for the same reason, to have had from myself the whole remainder of perfection, of the want of which I was conscious, and thus could of myself have become infinite, eternal, immutable, omniscient, all-powerful, and, in fine, have possessed all the perfections which I could recognize in God. For in order to know the nature of God (whose existence has been established by the preceding reasonings), as far as my own nature permitted, I had only to consider in reference to all the properties of which I found in my mind some idea, whether their possession was a mark of perfection; and I was assured that no one which indicated any imperfection was in him, and that none of the rest was awanting. Thus I perceived that doubt, inconstancy, sadness, and such like, could not be found in God, since I myself would have been happy to be free from them. Besides, I had ideas of many sensible and corporeal things; for although I might suppose that I was dreaming, and that all which I saw or imagined was false, I could not, nevertheless, deny that the ideas were in reality in my thoughts. But, because I had already very clearly recognized in myself that the intelligent nature is distinct from the corporeal, and as I observed that all composition is an evidence of dependency, and that a state of dependency is manifestly a state of imperfection, I therefore determined that it could not be a perfection in God to be compounded of these two natures and that consequently he was not so compounded; but that if there were any bodies in the world, or even any intelligences, or other natures that were not wholly perfect, their existence depended on his power in such a way that they could not subsist without him for a single moment.

I was disposed straightway to search for other truths and when I had represented to myself the object of the geometers, which I conceived to be a continuous body or a space indefinitely extended in length, breadth, and height or depth, divisible into divers parts which admit of different figures and sizes, and of being moved or transposed in all manner of ways (for all this the geometers suppose to be in the object they contemplate), I went over some of their simplest demonstrations. And, in the first place, I observed, that the great certitude which by common consent is accorded to these demonstrations, is founded solely upon this, that they are clearly conceived in accordance with the rules I have already laid down In the next place, I perceived that there was nothing at all in these demonstrations which could assure me of the existence of their object: thus, for example, supposing a triangle to be given, I distinctly perceived that its three angles were necessarily equal to two right angles, but I did not on that account perceive anything which could assure me that any triangle existed: while, on the contrary, recurring to the examination of the idea of a Perfect Being, I found that the existence of the Being was comprised in the idea in the same way that the equality of its three angles to two right angles is comprised in the idea of a triangle, or as in the idea of a sphere, the equidistance of all points on its surface from the center, or even still more clearly; and that consequently it is at least as certain that God, who is this Perfect Being, is, or exists, as any demonstration of geometry can be.

But the reason which leads many to persuade them selves that there is a difficulty in knowing this truth, and even also in knowing what their mind really is, is that they never raise their thoughts above sensible objects, and are so accustomed to consider nothing except by way of imagination, which is a mode of thinking limited to material objects, that all that is not imaginable seems to them not intelligible. The truth of this is sufficiently manifest from the single circumstance, that the philosophers of the schools accept as a maxim that there is nothing in the understanding which was not previously in the senses, in which however it is certain that the ideas of God and of the soul have never been; and it appears to me that they who make use of their imagination to comprehend these ideas do exactly the some thing as if, in order to hear sounds or smell odors, they strove to avail themselves of their eyes; unless indeed that there is this difference, that the sense of sight does not afford us an inferior assurance to those of smell or hearing; in place of which, neither our imagination nor our senses can give us assurance of anything unless our understanding intervene.

Finally, if there be still persons who are not sufficiently persuaded of the existence of God and of the soul, by the reasons I have adduced, I am desirous that they should know that all the other propositions, of the truth of which they deem themselves perhaps more assured, as that we have a body, and that there exist stars and an earth, and such like, are less certain; for, although we have a moral assurance of these things, which is so strong that there is an appearance of extravagance in doubting of their existence, yet at the same time no one, unless his intellect is impaired, can deny, when the question relates to a metaphysical certitude, that there is sufficient reason to exclude entire assurance, in the observation that when asleep we can in the same way imagine ourselves possessed of another body and that we see other stars and another earth, when there is nothing of the kind. For how do we know that the thoughts which occur in dreaming are false rather than those other which we experience when awake, since the former are often not less vivid and distinct than the latter? And though men of the highest genius study this question as long as they please, I do not believe that they will be able to give any reason which can be sufficient to remove this doubt, unless they presuppose the existence of God. For, in the first place even the principle which I have already taken as a rule, viz., that all the things which we clearly and distinctly conceive are true, is certain only because God is or exists and because he is a Perfect Being, and because all that we possess is derived from him: whence it follows that our ideas or notions, which to the extent of their clearness and distinctness are real, and proceed from God, must to that extent be true. Accordingly, whereas we not infrequently have ideas or notions in which some falsity is contained, this can only be the case with such as are to some extent confused and obscure, and in this proceed from nothing (participate of negation), that is, exist in us thus confused because we are not wholly perfect. And it is evident that it is not less repugnant that falsity or imperfection, in so far as it is imperfection, should proceed from God, than that truth or perfection should proceed from nothing. But if we did not know that all which we possess of real and true proceeds from a Perfect and Infinite Being, however clear and distinct our ideas might be, we should have no ground on that account for the assurance that they possessed the perfection of being true.

But after the knowledge of God and of the soul has rendered us certain of this rule, we can easily understand that the truth of the thoughts we experience when awake, ought not in the slightest degree to be called in question on account of the illusions of our dreams. For if it happened that an individual, even when asleep, had some very distinct idea, as, for example, if a geometer should discover some new demonstration, the circumstance of his being asleep would not militate against its truth; and as for the most ordinary error of our dreams, which consists in their representing to us various objects in the same way as our external senses, this is not prejudicial, since it leads us very properly to suspect the truth of the ideas of sense; for we are not infrequently deceived in the same manner when awake; as when persons in the jaundice see all objects yellow, or when the stars or bodies at a great distance appear to us much smaller than they are. For, in fine, whether awake or asleep, we ought never to allow ourselves to be persuaded of the truth of anything unless on the evidence of our reason. And it must be noted that I say of our reason, and not of our imagination or of our senses: thus, for example, although we very clearly see the sun, we ought not therefore to determine that it is only of the size which our sense of sight presents; and we may very distinctly imagine the head of a lion joined to the body of a goat, without being therefore shut up to the conclusion that a chimaera exists; for it is not a dictate of reason that what we thus see or imagine is in reality existent; but it plainly tells us that all our ideas or notions contain in them some truth; for otherwise it could not be that God, who is wholly perfect and veracious, should have placed them in us. And because our reasonings are never so clear or so complete during sleep as when we are awake, although sometimes the acts of our imagination are then as lively and distinct, if not more so than in our waking moments, reason further dictates that, since all our thoughts cannot be true because of our partial imperfection, those possessing truth must infallibly be found in the experience of our waking moments rather than in that of our dreams.

PART V

I would here willingly have proceeded to exhibit the whole chain of truths which I deduced from these primary but as with a view to this it would have been necessary now to treat of many questions in dispute among the earned, with whom I do not wish to be embroiled, I believe that it will be better for me to refrain from this exposition, and only mention in general what these truths are, that the more judicious may be able to determine whether a more special account of them would conduce to the public advantage. I have ever remained firm in my original resolution to suppose no other principle than that of which I have recently availed myself in demonstrating the existence of God and of the soul, and to accept as true nothing that did not appear to me more clear and certain than the demonstrations of the geometers had formerly appeared; and yet I venture to state that not only have I found means to satisfy myself in a short time on all the principal difficulties which are usually treated of in philosophy, but I have also observed certain laws established in nature by God in such a manner, and of which he has impressed on our minds such notions, that after we have reflected sufficiently upon these, we cannot doubt that they are accurately observed in all that exists or takes place in the world and farther, by considering the concatenation of these laws, it appears to me that I have discovered many truths more useful and more important than all I had before learned, or even had expected to learn.

But because I have essayed to expound the chief of these discoveries in a treatise which certain considerations prevent me from publishing, I cannot make the results known more conveniently than by here giving a summary of the contents of this treatise. It was my design to comprise in it all that, before I set myself to write it, I thought I knew of the nature of material objects. But like the painters who, finding themselves unable to represent equally well on a plain surface all the different faces of a solid body, select one of the chief, on which alone they make the light fall, and throwing the rest into the shade, allow them to appear only in so far as they can be seen while looking at the principal one; so, fearing lest I should not be able to compense in my discourse all that was in my mind, I resolved to expound singly, though at considerable length, my opinions regarding light; then to take the opportunity of adding something on the sun and the fixed stars, since light almost wholly proceeds from them; on the heavens since they transmit it; on the planets, comets, and earth, since they reflect it; and particularly on all the bodies that are upon the earth, since they are either colored, or transparent, or luminous; and finally on man, since he is the spectator of these objects. Further, to enable me to cast this variety of subjects somewhat into the shade, and to express my judgment regarding them with greater freedom, without being necessitated to adopt or refute the opinions of the learned, I resolved to leave all the people here to their disputes, and to speak only of what would happen in a new world, if God were now to create somewhere in the imaginary spaces matter sufficient to compose one, and were to agitate variously and confusedly the different parts of this matter, so that there resulted a chaos as disordered as the poets ever feigned, and after that did nothing more than lend his ordinary concurrence to nature, and allow her to act in accordance with the laws which he had established. On this supposition, I, in the first place, described this matter, and essayed to represent it in such a manner that to my mind there can be nothing clearer and more intelligible, except what has been recently said regarding God and the soul; for I even expressly supposed that it possessed none of those forms or qualities which are so debated in the schools, nor in general anything the knowledge of which is not so natural to our minds that no one can so much as imagine himself ignorant of it. Besides, I have pointed out what are the laws of nature; and, with no other principle upon which to found my reasonings except the infinite perfection of God, I endeavored to demonstrate all those about which there could be any room for doubt, and to prove that they are such, that even if God had created more worlds, there could have been none in which these laws were not observed. Thereafter, I showed how the greatest part of the matter of this chaos must, in accordance with these laws, dispose and arrange itself in such a way as to present the appearance of heavens; how in the meantime some of its parts must compose an earth and some planets and comets, and others a sun and fixed stars. And, making a digression at this stage on the subject of light, I expounded at considerable length what the nature of that light must be which is found in the sun and the stars, and how thence in an instant of time it traverses the immense spaces of the heavens, and how from the planets and comets it is reflected towards the earth. To this I likewise added much respecting the substance, the situation, the motions, and all the different qualities of these heavens and stars; so that I thought I had said enough respecting them to show that there is nothing observable in the heavens or stars of our system that must not, or at least may not appear precisely alike in those of the system which I described. I came next to speak of the earth in particular, and to show how, even though I had expressly supposed that God had given no weight to the matter of which it is composed, this should not prevent all its parts from tending exactly to its center; how with water and air on its surface, the disposition of the heavens and heavenly bodies, more especially of the moon, must cause a flow and ebb, like in all its circumstances to that observed in our seas, as also a certain current both of water and air from east to west, such as is likewise observed between the tropics; how the mountains, seas, fountains, and rivers might naturally be formed in it, and the metals produced in the mines, and the plants grow in the fields and in general, how all the bodies which are commonly denominated mixed or composite might be generated and, among other things in the discoveries alluded to inasmuch as besides the stars, I knew nothing except fire which produces light, I spared no pains to set forth all that pertains to its nature,—the manner of its production and support, and to explain how heat is sometimes found without light, and light without heat; to show how it can induce various colors upon different bodies and other diverse qualities; how it reduces some to a liquid state and hardens others; how it can consume almost all bodies, or convert them into ashes and smoke; and finally, how from these ashes, by the mere intensity of its action, it forms glass: for as this transmutation of ashes into glass appeared to me as wonderful as any other in nature, I took a special pleasure in describing it. I was not, however, disposed, from these circumstances, to conclude that this world had been created in the manner I described; for it is much more likely that God made it at the first such as it was to be. But this is certain, and an opinion commonly received among theologians, that the action by which he now sustains it is the same with that by which he originally created it; so that even although he had from the beginning given it no other form than that of chaos, provided only he had established certain laws of nature, and had lent it his concurrence to enable it to act as it is wont to do, it may be believed, without discredit to the miracle of creation, that, in this way alone, things purely material might, in course of time, have become such as we observe them at present; and their nature is much more easily conceived when they are beheld coming in this manner gradually into existence, than when they are only considered as produced at once in a finished and perfect state.

From the description of inanimate bodies and plants, I passed to animals, and particularly to man. But since I had not as yet sufficient knowledge to enable me to treat of these in the same manner as of the rest, that is to say, by deducing effects from their causes, and by showing from what elements and in what manner nature must produce them, I remained satisfied with the supposition that God formed the body of man wholly like to one of ours, as well in the external shape of the members as in the internal conformation of the organs, of the same matter with that I had described, and at first placed in it no rational soul, nor any other principle, in room of the vegetative or sensitive soul, beyond kindling in the heart one of those fires without light, such as I had already described, and which I thought was not different from the heat in hay that has been heaped together before it is dry, or that which causes fermentation in new wines before they are run clear of the fruit. For, when I examined the kind of functions which might, as consequences of this supposition, exist in this body, I found precisely all those which may exist in us independently of all power of thinking, and consequently without being in any measure owing to the soul; in other words, to that part of us which is distinct from the body, and of which it has been said above that the nature distinctively consists in thinking, functions in which the animals void of reason may be said wholly to resemble us; but among which I could not discover any of those that, as dependent on thought alone, belong to us as men, while, on the other hand, I did afterwards discover these as soon as I supposed God to have created a rational soul, and to have annexed it to this body in a particular manner which I described.

But, in order to show how I there handled this matter, I mean here to give the explication of the motion of the heart and arteries, which, as the first and most general motion observed in animals, will afford the means of readily determining what should be thought of all the rest. And that there may be less difficulty in understanding what I am about to say on this subject, I advise those who are not versed in anatomy, before they commence the perusal of these observations, to take the trouble of getting dissected in their presence the heart of some large animal possessed of lungs (for this is throughout sufficiently like the human), and to have shown to them its two ventricles or cavities: in the first place, that in the right side, with which correspond two very ample tubes, viz., the hollow vein (*vena cava*), which is the principal receptacle of the blood, and the trunk of the tree, as it were, of which all the other veins in the body are branches; and the arterial vein (*vena arteriosa*), inappropriately so denominated, since it is in truth only an artery, which, taking its rise in the heart, is divided, after passing out from it, into many branches which presently disperse themselves all over the lungs; in the second place, the cavity in the left side, with which correspond in the same manner two canals in size equal to or larger than the preceding, viz., the venous artery (*arteria venosa*), likewise inappropriately thus designated, because it is simply a vein which comes from the lungs, where it is divided into many branches, interlaced with those of the arterial vein, and those of the tube called the windpipe, through which the air we breathe enters; and the great artery which, issuing from the heart, sends its branches all over the body. I should wish also that such persons were carefully shown the eleven pellicles which, like so many small valves, open and shut the four orifices that are in these two cavities, viz., three at the entrance of the hollow veins where they are disposed in such a manner as by no means to prevent the blood which it contains from flowing into the right ventricle of the heart, and yet exactly to prevent its flowing out; three at the entrance to the arterial vein, which, arranged in a manner exactly the opposite of the former, readily permit the blood contained in this cavity to pass into the lungs, but hinder that contained in the lungs from returning to this cavity; and, in like manner, two others at the mouth of the venous artery, which allow the blood from the lungs to flow into the left cavity of the heart, but preclude its return; and three at the mouth of the great artery, which suffer the blood to flow from the heart, but prevent its reflux. Nor do we need to seek any other reason for the number of these pellicles beyond this that the orifice of the venous artery being of an oval shape from the nature of its situation, can be adequately closed with two, whereas the others being round are more conveniently closed with three. Besides, I wish such persons to observe that the grand artery and the arterial vein are of much harder and firmer texture than the venous artery and the hollow vein; and that the two last expand before entering the heart, and there form, as it were, two pouches denominated the auricles of the heart, which are composed of a substance similar to that of the heart itself; and that there is always more warmth in the heart than in any other part of the body—and finally, that this heat is capable of causing any drop of blood that passes into the cavities rapidly to expand and dilate, just as all liquors do when allowed to fall drop by drop into a highly heated vessel.

For, after these things, it is not necessary for me to say anything more with a view to explain the motion of the heart, except that when its cavities are not full of blood, into these the blood of necessity flows,—from the hollow vein into the right, and from the venous artery into the left; because these two vessels are always full of blood, and their orifices, which are turned towards the heart, cannot then be closed. But as soon as two drops of blood have thus passed, one into each of the cavities, these drops which cannot but be very large, because the orifices through which they pass are wide, and the vessels from which they come full of blood, are immediately rarefied, and dilated by the heat they meet with. In this way they cause the whole heart to expand, and at the same time press home and shut the five small valves that are at the entrances of the two vessels from which they flow, and thus prevent any more blood from coming down into the heart, and becoming more and more rarefied, they push open the six small valves that are in the orifices of the other two vessels, through which they pass out, causing in this way all the branches of the arterial vein and of the grand artery to expand almost simultaneously with the heart which immediately thereafter begins to contract, as do also the arteries, because the blood that has entered them has cooled, and the six small valves close, and the five of the hollow vein and of the venous artery open anew and allow a passage to other two drops of blood, which cause the heart and the arteries again to expand as before. And, because the blood which thus enters into the heart passes through these two pouches called auricles, it thence happens that their motion is the contrary of that of the heart, and that when it expands they contract. But lest those who are ignorant of the force of mathematical demonstrations and who are not accustomed to distinguish true reasons from mere verisimilitudes, should venture, without examination, to deny what has been said, I wish it to be considered that the motion which I have now explained follows as necessarily from the very arrangement of the parts, which may be observed in the heart by the eye alone, and from the heat which may be felt with the fingers, and from the nature of the blood as learned from experience, as does the motion of a clock from the power, the situation, and shape of its counterweights and wheels.

But if it be asked how it happens that the blood in the veins, flowing in this way continually into the heart, is not exhausted, and why the arteries do not become too full, since all the blood which passes through the heart flows into them, I need only mention in reply what has been written by a physician of England, who has the honor of having broken the ice on this subject, and of having been the first to teach that there are many small passages at the extremities of the arteries, through which the blood received by them from the heart passes into the small branches of the veins, whence it again returns to the heart; so that its course amounts precisely to a perpetual circulation. Of this we have abundant proof in the ordinary experience of surgeons, who, by binding the arm with a tie of moderate straitness above the part where they open the vein, cause the blood to flow more copiously than it would have done without any ligature; whereas quite the contrary would happen were they to bind it below; that is, between the hand and the opening, or were to make the ligature above the opening very tight. For it is manifest that the tie, moderately straightened, while adequate to hinder the blood already in the arm from returning towards the heart by the veins, cannot on that account prevent new blood from coming forward through the arteries, because these are situated below the veins, and their coverings, from their greater consistency, are more difficult to compress; and also that the blood which comes from the heart tends to pass through them to the hand with greater force than it does to return from the hand to the heart through the veins. And since the latter current escapes from the arm by the opening made in one of the veins, there must of necessity be certain passages below the ligature, that is, towards the extremities of the arm through which it can come thither from the arteries. This physician likewise abundantly establishes what he has advanced respecting the motion of the blood, from the existence of certain pellicles, so disposed in various places along the course of the veins, in the manner of small valves, as not to permit the blood to pass from the middle of the body towards the extremities, but only to return from the extremities to the heart; and farther, from experience which shows that all the blood which is in the body may flow out of it in a very short time through a single artery that has been cut, even although this had been closely tied in the immediate neighborhood of the heart and cut between the heart and the ligature, so as to prevent the supposition that the blood flowing out of it could come from any other quarter than the heart.

But there are many other circumstances which evince that what I have alleged is the true cause of the motion of the blood: thus, in the first place, the difference that is observed between the blood which flows from the veins, and that from the arteries, can only arise from this, that being rarefied, and, as it were, distilled by passing through the heart, it is thinner, and more vivid, and warmer immediately after leaving the heart, in other words, when in the arteries, than it was a short time before passing into either, in other words, when it was in the veins; and if attention be given, it will be found that this difference is very marked only in the neighborhood of the heart; and is not so evident in parts more remote from it.

In the next place, the consistency of the coats of which the arterial vein and the great artery are composed, sufficiently shows that the blood is impelled against them with more force than against the veins. And why should the left cavity of the heart and the great artery be wider and larger than the right cavity and the arterial vein, were it not that the blood of the venous artery, having only been in the lungs after it has passed through the heart, is thinner, and rarefies more readily, and in a higher degree, than the blood which proceeds immediately from the hollow vein? And what can physicians conjecture from feeling the pulse unless they know that according as the blood changes its nature it can be rarefied by the warmth of the heart, in a higher or lower degree, and more or less quickly than before? And if it be inquired how this heat is communicated to the other members, must it not be admitted that this is effected by means of the blood, which, passing through the heart, is there heated anew, and thence diffused over all the body? Whence it happens, that if the blood be withdrawn from any part, the heat is likewise withdrawn by the same means; and although the heart were as-hot as glowing iron, it would not be capable of warming the feet and hands as at present, unless it continually sent thither new blood. We likewise perceive from this, that the true use of respiration is to bring sufficient fresh air into the lungs, to cause the blood which flows into them from the right ventricle of the heart, where it has been rarefied and, as it were, changed into vapors, to become thick, and to convert it anew into blood, before it flows into the left cavity, without which process it would be unfit for the nourishment of the fire that is there. This receives confirmation from the circumstance, that it is observed of animals destitute of lungs that they have also but one cavity in the heart, and that in children who cannot use them while in the womb, there is a hole through which the blood flows from the hollow vein into the left cavity of the heart, and a tube through which it passes from the arterial vein into the grand artery without passing through the lung. In the next place, how could digestion be carried on in the stomach unless the heart communicated heat to it through the arteries, and along with this certain of the more fluid parts of the blood, which assist in the dissolution of the food that has been taken in? Is not also the operation which converts the juice of food into blood easily comprehended, when it is considered that it is distilled by passing and repassing through the heart perhaps more than one or two hundred times in a day? And what more need be adduced to explain nutrition, and the production of the different humors of the body, beyond saying, that the force with which the blood, in being rarefied, passes from the heart towards the extremities of the arteries, causes certain of its parts to remain in the members at which they arrive, and there occupy the place of some others expelled by them; and that according to the situation, shape, or smallness of the pores with which they meet, some rather than others flow into certain parts, in the same way that some sieves are observed to act, which, by being variously perforated, serve to separate different species of grain? And, in the last place, what above all is here worthy of observation, is the generation of the animal spirits, which are like a very subtle wind, or rather a very pure and vivid flame which, continually ascending in great abundance from the heart to the brain, thence penetrates through the nerves into the muscles, and gives motion to all the members; so that to account for other parts of the blood which, as most agitated and penetrating, are the fittest to compose these spirits, proceeding towards the brain, it is not necessary to suppose any other cause, than simply, that the arteries which carry them thither proceed from the heart in the most direct lines, and that, according to the rules of mechanics which are the same with those of nature, when many objects tend at once to the same point where there is not sufficient room for all (as is the case with the parts of the blood which flow forth from the left cavity of the heart and tend towards the brain), the weaker and less agitated parts must necessarily be driven aside from that point by the stronger which alone in this way reach it I had expounded all these matters with sufficient minuteness in the treatise which I formerly thought of publishing. And after these, I had shown what must be the fabric of the nerves and muscles of the human body to give the animal spirits contained in it the power to move the members, as when we see heads shortly after they have been struck off still move and bite the earth, although no longer animated; what changes must take place in the brain to produce waking, sleep, and dreams; how light, sounds, odors, tastes, heat, and all the other qualities of external objects impress it with different ideas by means of the senses; how hunger, thirst, and the other internal affections can likewise impress upon it divers ideas; what must be understood by the common sense (*sensus communis*) in which these ideas are received, by the memory which retains them, by the fantasy which can change them in various ways, and out of them compose new ideas, and which, by the same means, distributing the animal spirits through the muscles, can cause the members of such a body to move in as many different ways, and in a manner as suited, whether to the objects that are presented to its senses or to its internal affections, as can take place in our own case apart from the guidance of the will. Nor will this appear at all strange to those who are acquainted with the variety of movements performed by the different automata, or moving machines fabricated by human industry, and that with help of but few pieces compared with the great multitude of bones, muscles, nerves, arteries, veins, and other parts that are found in the body of each animal. Such persons will look upon this body as a machine made by the hands of God, which is incomparably better arranged, and adequate to movements more admirable than is any machine of human invention. And here I specially stayed to show that, were there such machines exactly resembling organs and outward form an ape or any other irrational animal, we could have no means of knowing that they were in any respect of a different nature from these animals; but if there were machines bearing the image of our bodies, and capable of imitating our actions as far as it is morally possible, there would still remain two most certain tests whereby to know that they were not therefore really men. Of these the first is that they could never use words or other signs arranged in such a manner as is competent to us in order to declare our thoughts to others: for we may easily conceive a machine to be so constructed that it emits vocables, and even that it emits some correspondent to the action upon it of external objects which cause a change in its organs; for example, if touched in a particular place it may demand what we wish to say to it; if in another it may cry out that it is hurt, and such like; but not that it should arrange them variously so as appositely to reply to what is said in its presence, as men of the lowest grade of intellect can do. The second test is, that although such machines might execute many things with equal or perhaps greater perfection than any of us, they would, without doubt, fail in certain others from which it could be discovered that they did not act from knowledge, but solely from the disposition of their organs: for while reason is an universal instrument that is alike available on every occasion, these organs, on the contrary, need a particular arrangement for each particular action; whence it must be morally impossible that there should exist in any machine a diversity of organs sufficient to enable it to act in all the occurrences of life, in the way in which our reason enables us to act. Again, by means of these two tests we may likewise know the difference between men and brutes. For it is highly deserving of remark, that there are no men so dull and stupid, not even idiots, as to be incapable of joining together different words, and thereby constructing a declaration by which to make their thoughts understood; and that on the other hand, there is no other animal, however perfect or happily circumstanced, which can do the like. Nor does this inability arise from want of organs: for we observe that magpies and parrots can utter words like ourselves, and are yet unable to speak as we do, that is, so as to show that they understand what they say; in place of which men born deaf and dumb, and thus not less, but rather more than the brutes, destitute of the organs which others use in speaking, are in the habit of spontaneously inventing certain signs by which they discover their thoughts to those who, being usually in their company, have leisure to learn their language. And this proves not only that the brutes have less reason than man, but that they have none at all: for we see that very little is required to enable a person to speak; and since a certain inequality of capacity is observable among animals of the same species, as well as among men, and since some are more capable of being instructed than others, it is incredible that the most perfect ape or parrot of its species, should not in this be equal to the most stupid infant of its kind or at least to one that was crack-brained, unless the soul of brutes were of a nature wholly different from ours. And we ought not to confound speech with the natural movements which indicate the passions, and can be imitated by machines as well as manifested by animals; nor must it be thought with certain of the ancients, that the brutes speak, although we do not understand their language. For if such were the case, since they are endowed with many organs analogous to ours, they could as easily communicate their thoughts to us as to their fellows. It is also very worthy of remark, that, though there are many animals which manifest more industry than we in certain of their actions, the same animals are yet observed to show none at all in many others: so that the circumstance that they do better than we does not prove that they are endowed with mind, for it would thence follow that they possessed greater reason than any of us, and could surpass us in all things; on the contrary, it rather proves that they are destitute of reason, and that it is nature which acts in them according to the disposition of their organs: thus it is seen, that a clock composed only of wheels and weights can number the hours and measure time more exactly than we with all our skin.

I had after this described the reasonable soul, and shown that it could by no means be educed from the power of matter, as the other things of which I had spoken, but that it must be expressly created; and that it is not sufficient that it be lodged in the human body exactly like a pilot in a ship, unless perhaps to move its members, but that it is necessary for it to be joined and united more closely to the body, in order to have sensations and appetites similar to ours, and thus constitute a real man. I here entered, in conclusion, upon the subject of the soul at considerable length, because it is of the greatest moment: for after the error of those who deny the existence of God, an error which I think I have already sufficiently refuted, there is none that is more powerful in leading feeble minds astray from the straight path of virtue than the supposition that the soul of the brutes is of the same nature with our own;

and consequently that after this life we have nothing to hope for or fear, more than flies and ants; in place of which, when we know how far they differ we much better comprehend the reasons which establish that the soul is of a nature wholly independent of the body, and that consequently it is not liable to die with the latter and, finally, because no other causes are observed capable of destroying it, we are naturally led thence to judge that it is immortal.

PART VI

Three years have now elapsed since I finished the treatise containing all these matters; and I was beginning to revise it, with the view to put it into the hands of a printer, when I learned that persons to whom I greatly defer, and whose authority over my actions is hardly less influential than is my own reason over my thoughts, had condemned a certain doctrine in physics, published a short time previously by another individual to which I will not say that I adhered, but only that, previously to their censure I had observed in it nothing which I could imagine to be prejudicial either to religion or to the state, and nothing therefore which would have prevented me from giving expression to it in writing, if reason had persuaded me of its truth; and this led me to fear lest among my own doctrines likewise some one might be found in which I had departed from the truth, notwithstanding the great care I have always taken not to accord belief to new opinions of which I had not the most certain demonstrations, and not to give expression to aught that might tend to the hurt of any one. This has been sufficient to make me alter my purpose of publishing them; for although the reasons by which I had been induced to take this resolution were very strong, yet my inclination, which has always been hostile to writing books, enabled me immediately to discover other considerations sufficient to excuse me for not undertaking the task. And these reasons, on one side and the other, are such, that not only is it in some measure my interest here to state them, but that of the public, perhaps, to know them.

I have never made much account of what has proceeded from my own mind; and so long as I gathered no other advantage from the method I employ beyond satisfying myself on some difficulties belonging to the speculative sciences, or endeavoring to regulate my actions according to the principles it taught me, I never thought myself bound to publish anything respecting it. For in what regards manners, every one is so full of his own wisdom, that there might be found as many reformers as heads, if any were allowed to take upon themselves the task of mending them, except those whom God has constituted the supreme rulers of his people or to whom he has given sufficient grace and zeal to be prophets; and although my speculations greatly pleased myself, I believed that others had theirs, which perhaps pleased them still more. But as soon as I had acquired some general notions respecting physics, and beginning to make trial of them in various particular difficulties, had observed how far they can carry us, and how much they differ from the principles that have been employed up to the present time, I believed that I could not keep them concealed without sinning grievously against the law by which we are bound to promote, as far as in us lies, the general good of mankind. For by them I perceived it to be possible to arrive at knowledge highly useful in life; and in room of the speculative philosophy usually taught in the schools, to discover a practical, by means of which, knowing the force and action of fire, water, air the stars, the heavens, and all the other bodies that surround us, as distinctly as we know the various crafts of our artisans, we might also apply them in the same way to all the uses to which they are adapted, and thus render ourselves the lords and possessors of nature. And this is a result to be desired, not only in order to the invention of an infinity of arts, by which we might be enabled to enjoy without any trouble the fruits of the earth, and all its comforts, but also and especially for the preservation of health, which is without doubt, of all the blessings of this life, the first and fundamental one; for the mind is so intimately dependent upon the condition and relation of the organs of the body, that if any means can ever be found to render men wiser and more ingenious than hitherto, I believe that it is in medicine they must be sought for. It is true that the science of medicine, as it now exists, contains few things whose utility is very remarkable: but without any wish to depreciate it, I am confident that there is no one, even among those whose profession it is, who does not admit that all at present known in it is almost nothing in comparison of what remains to be discovered; and that we could free ourselves from an infinity of maladies of body as well as of mind, and perhaps also even from the debility of age, if we had sufficiently ample knowledge of their causes, and of all the remedies provided for us by nature. But since I designed to employ my whole life in the search after so necessary a science, and since I had fallen in with a path which seems to me such, that if any one follow it he must inevitably reach the end desired, unless he be hindered either by the shortness of life or the want of experiments, I judged that there could be no more effectual provision against these two impediments than if I were faithfully to communicate to the public all the little I might myself have found, and incite men of superior genius to strive to proceed farther, by contributing, each according to his inclination and ability, to the experiments which it would be necessary to make, and also by informing the public of all they might discover, so that, by the last beginning where those before them had left off, and thus connecting the lives and labours of many, we might collectively proceed much farther than each by himself could do.

I remarked, moreover, with respect to experiments, that they become always more necessary the more one is advanced in knowledge; for, at the commencement, it is better to make use only of what is spontaneously presented to our senses, and of which we cannot remain ignorant, provided we bestow on it any reflection, however slight, than to concern ourselves about more uncommon and recondite phenomena: the reason of which is, that the more uncommon often only mislead us so long as the causes of the more ordinary are still unknown; and the circumstances upon which they depend are almost always so special and minute as to be highly difficult to detect. But in this I have adopted the following order: first, I have essayed to find in general the principles, or first causes of all that is or can be in the world, without taking into consideration for this end anything but God himself who has created it, and without educing them from any other source than from certain germs of truths naturally existing in our minds In the second place, I examined what were the first and most ordinary effects that could be deduced from these causes; and it appears to me that, in this way, I have found heavens, stars, an earth, and even on the earth water, air, fire, minerals, and some other things of this kind, which of all others are the most common and simple, and hence the easiest to know. Afterwards when I wished to descend to the more particular, so many diverse objects presented themselves to me, that I believed it to be impossible for the human mind to distinguish the forms or species of bodies that are upon the earth, from an infinity of others which might have been, if it had pleased God to place them there, or consequently to apply them to our use, unless we rise to causes through their effects, and avail ourselves of many particular experiments. Thereupon, turning over in my mind I the objects that had ever been presented to my senses I freely venture to state that I have never observed any which I could not satisfactorily explain by the principles had discovered. But it is necessary also to confess that the power of nature is so ample and vast, and these principles so simple and general, that I have hardly observed a single particular effect which I cannot at once recognize as capable of being deduced in man different modes from the principles, and that my greatest difficulty usually is to discover in which of these modes the effect is dependent upon them; for out of this difficulty cannot otherwise extricate myself than by again seeking certain experiments, which may be such that their result is not the same, if it is in the one of these modes at we must explain it, as it would be if it were to be explained in the other. As to what remains, I am now in a position to discern, as I think, with sufficient clearness what course must be taken to make the majority those experiments which may conduce to this end: but I perceive likewise that they are such and so numerous, that neither my hands nor my income, though it were a thousand times larger than it is, would be sufficient for them all; so that according as henceforward I shall have the means of making more or fewer experiments, I shall in the same proportion make greater or less progress in the knowledge of nature. This was what I had hoped to make known by the treatise I had written, and so clearly to exhibit the advantage that would thence accrue to the public, as to induce all who have the common good of man at heart, that is, all who are virtuous in truth, and not merely in appearance, or according to opinion, as well to communicate to me the experiments they had already made, as to assist me in those that remain to be made.

But since that time other reasons have occurred to me, by which I have been led to change my opinion, and to think that I ought indeed to go on committing to writing all the results which I deemed of any moment, as soon as I should have tested their truth, and to bestow the same care upon them as I would have done had it been my design to publish them. This course commended itself to me, as well because I thus afforded myself more ample inducement to examine them thoroughly, for doubtless that is always more narrowly scrutinized which we believe will be read by many, than that which is written merely for our private use (and frequently what has seemed to me true when I first conceived it, has appeared false when I have set about committing it to writing), as because I thus lost no opportunity of advancing the interests of the public, as far as in me lay, and since thus likewise, if my writings possess any value, those into whose hands they may fall after my death may be able to put them to what use they deem proper. But I resolved by no means to consent to their publication during my lifetime, lest either the oppositions or the controversies to which they might give rise, or even the reputation, such as it might be, which they would acquire for me, should be any occasion of my losing the time that I had set apart for my own improvement. For though it be true that every one is bound to promote to the extent of his ability the good of others, and that to be useful to no one is really to be worthless, yet it is likewise true that our cares ought to extend beyond the present, and it is good to omit doing what might perhaps bring some profit to the living, when we have in view the accomplishment of other ends that will be of much greater advantage to posterity. And in truth, I am quite willing it should be known that the little I have hitherto learned is almost nothing in comparison with that of which I am ignorant, and to the knowledge of which I do not despair of being able to attain; for it is much the same with those who gradually discover truth in the sciences, as with those who when growing rich find less difficulty in making great acquisitions, than they formerly experienced when poor in making acquisitions of much smaller amount. Or they may be compared to the commanders of armies, whose forces usually increase in proportion to their victories, and who need greater prudence to keep together the residue of their troops after a defeat than after a victory to take towns and provinces. For he truly engages in battle who endeavors to surmount all the difficulties and errors which prevent him from reaching the knowledge of truth, and he is overcome in fight who admits a false opinion touching a matter of any generality and importance, and he requires thereafter much more skill to recover his former position than to make great advances when once in possession of thoroughly ascertained principles. As for myself, if I have succeeded in discovering any truths in the sciences (and I trust that what is contained in this volume I will show that I have found some), I can declare that they are but the consequences and results of five or six principal difficulties which I have surmounted, and my encounters with which I reckoned as battles in which victory declared for me. I will not hesitate even to avow my belief that nothing further is wanting to enable me fully to realize my designs than to gain two or three similar victories; and that I am not so far advanced in years but that, according to the ordinary course of nature, I may still have sufficient leisure for this end. But I conceive myself the more bound to husband the time that remains the greater my expectation of being able to employ it aright, and I should doubtless have much to rob me of it, were I to publish the principles of my physics: for although they are almost all so evident that to assent to them no more is needed than simply to understand them, and although there is not one of them of which I do not expect to be able to give demonstration, yet, as it is impossible that they can be in accordance with all the diverse opinions of others, I foresee that I should frequently be turned aside from my grand design, on occasion of the opposition which they would be sure to awaken.

It may be said, that these oppositions would be useful both in making me aware of my errors, and, if my speculations contain anything of value, in bringing others to a fuller understanding of it; and still farther, as many can see better than one, in leading others who are now beginning to avail themselves of my principles, to assist me in turn with their discoveries. But though I recognize my extreme liability to error, and scarce ever trust to the first thoughts which occur to me, yet-the experience I have had of possible objections to my views prevents me from anticipating any profit from them. For I have already had frequent proof of the judgments, as well of those I esteemed friends, as of some others to whom I thought I was an object of indifference, and even of some whose malignancy and envy would, I knew, determine them to endeavor to discover what partiality concealed from the eyes of my friends. But it has rarely happened that anything has been objected to me which I had myself altogether overlooked, unless it were something far removed from the subject: so that I have never met with a single critic of my opinions who did not appear to me either less rigorous or less equitable than myself. And further, I have never observed that any truth before unknown has been brought to light by the disputations that are practised in the schools; for while each strives for the victory, each is much more occupied in making the best of mere verisimilitude, than in weighing the reasons on both sides of the question; and those who have been long good advocates are not afterwards on that account the better judges.

As for the advantage that others would derive from the communication of my thoughts, it could not be very great; because I have not yet so far prosecuted them as that much does not remain to be added before they can be applied to practice. And I think I may say without vanity, that if there is any one who can carry them out that length, it must be myself rather than another: not that there may not be in the world many minds incomparably superior to mine, but because one cannot so well seize a thing and make it one's own, when it has been learned from another, as when one has himself discovered it. And so true is this of the present subject that, though I have often explained some of my opinions to persons of much acuteness, who, whilst I was speaking, appeared to understand them very distinctly, yet, when they repeated them, I have observed that they almost always changed them to such an extent that I could no longer acknowledge them as mine. I am glad, by the way, to take this opportunity of requesting posterity never to believe on hearsay that anything has proceeded from me which has not been published by myself; and I am not at all astonished at the extravagances attributed to those ancient philosophers whose own writings we do not possess; whose thoughts, however, I do not on that account suppose to have been really absurd, seeing they were among the ablest men of their times, but only that these have been falsely represented to us. It is observable, accordingly, that scarcely in a single instance has any one of their disciples surpassed them; and I am quite sure that the most devoted of the present followers of Aristotle would think themselves happy if they had as much knowledge of nature as he possessed, were it even under the condition that they should never afterwards attain to higher. In this respect they are like the ivy which never strives to rise above the tree that sustains it, and which frequently even returns downwards when it has reached the top; for it seems to me that they also sink, in other words, render themselves less wise than they would be if they gave up study, who, not contented with knowing all that is intelligibly explained in their author, desire in addition to find in him the solution of many difficulties of which he says not a word, and never perhaps so much as thought. Their fashion of philosophizing, however, is well suited to persons whose abilities fall below mediocrity; for the obscurity of the distinctions and principles of which they make use enables them to speak of all things with as much confidence as if they really knew them, and to defend all that they say on any subject against the most subtle and skillful, without its being possible for any one to convict them of error. In this they seem to me to be like a blind man, who, in order to fight on equal terms with a person that sees, should have made him descend to the bottom of an intensely dark cave: and I may say that such persons have an interest in my refraining from publishing the principles of the philosophy of which I make use; for, since these are of a kind the simplest and most evident, I should, by publishing them, do much the same as if I were to throw open the windows, and allow the light of day to enter the cave into which the combatants had descended. But even superior men have no reason for any great anxiety to know these principles, for if what they desire is to be able to speak of all things, and to acquire a reputation for learning, they will gain their end more easily by remaining satisfied with the appearance of truth, which can be found without much difficulty in all sorts of matters, than by seeking the truth itself which unfolds itself but slowly and that only in some departments, while it obliges us, when we have to speak of others, freely to confess our ignorance. If, however, they prefer the knowledge of some few truths to the vanity of appearing ignorant of none, as such knowledge is undoubtedly much to be preferred, and, if they choose to follow a course similar to mine, they do not require for this that I should say anything more than I have already said in this discourse. For if they are capable of making greater advancement than I have made, they will much more be able of themselves to discover all that I believe myself to have found; since as I have never examined aught except in order, it is certain that what yet remains to be discovered is in itself more difficult and recondite, than that which I have already been enabled to find, and the gratification would be much less in learning it from me than in discovering it for themselves. Besides this, the habit which they will acquire, by seeking first what is easy, and then passing onward slowly and step by step to the more difficult, will benefit them more than all my instructions. Thus, in my own case, I am persuaded that if I had been taught from my youth all the truths of which I have since sought out demonstrations, and had thus learned them without labour, I should never, perhaps, have known any beyond these; at least, I should never have acquired the habit and the facility which I think I possess in always discovering new truths in proportion as I give myself to the search. And, in a single word, if there is any work in the world which cannot be so well finished by another as by him who has commenced it, it is that at which I labour.

It is true, indeed, as regards the experiments which may conduce to this end, that one man is not equal to the task of making them all; but yet he can advantageously avail himself, in this work, of no hands besides his own, unless those of artisans, or parties of the same kind, whom he could pay, and whom the hope of gain (a means of great efficacy) might stimulate to accuracy in the performance of what was prescribed to them. For as to those who, through curiosity or a desire of learning, of their own accord, perhaps, offer him their services, besides that in general their promises exceed their performance, and that they sketch out fine designs of which not one is ever realized, they will, without doubt, expect to be compensated for their trouble by the explication of some difficulties, or, at least, by compliments and useless speeches, in which he cannot spend any portion of his time without loss to himself. And as for the experiments that others have already made, even although these parties should be willing of themselves to communicate them to him (which is what those who esteem them secrets will never do), the experiments are, for the most part, accompanied with so many circumstances and superfluous elements, as to make it exceedingly difficult to disentangle the truth from its adjuncts—besides, he will find almost all of them so ill described, or even so false (because those who made them have wished to see in them only such facts as they deemed conformable to their principles), that, if in the entire number there should be some of a nature suited to his purpose, still their value could not compensate for the time what would be necessary to make the selection. So that if there existed any one whom we assuredly knew to be capable of making discoveries of the highest kind, and of the greatest possible utility to the public; and if all other men were therefore eager by all means to assist him in successfully prosecuting his designs, I do not see that they could do aught else for him beyond contributing to defray the expenses of the experiments that might be necessary; and for the rest, prevent his being deprived of his leisure by the unseasonable interruptions of any one. But besides that I neither have so high an opinion of myself as to be willing to make promise of anything extraordinary, nor feed on imaginations so vain as to fancy that the public must be much interested in my designs; I do not, on the other hand, own a soul so mean as to be capable of accepting from any one a favor of which it could be supposed that I was unworthy.

These considerations taken together were the reason why, for the last three years, I have been unwilling to publish the treatise I had on hand, and why I even resolved to give publicity during my life to no other that was so general, or by which the principles of my physics might be understood. But since then, two other reasons have come into operation that have determined me here to subjoin some particular specimens, and give the public some account of my doings and designs. Of these considerations, the first is, that if I failed to do so, many who were cognizant of my previous intention to publish some writings, might have imagined that the reasons which induced me to refrain from so doing, were less to my credit than they really are; for although I am not immoderately desirous of glory, or even, if I may venture so to say, although I am averse from it in so far as I deem it hostile to repose which I hold in greater account than aught else, yet, at the same time, I have never sought to conceal my actions as if they were crimes, nor made use of many precautions that I might remain unknown; and this partly because I should have thought such a course of conduct a wrong against myself, and partly because it would have occasioned me some sort of uneasiness which would again have been contrary to the perfect mental tranquillity which I court. And forasmuch as, while thus indifferent to the thought alike of fame or of forgetfulness, I have yet been unable to prevent myself from acquiring some sort of reputation, I have thought it incumbent on me to do my best to save myself at least from being ill-spoken of. The other reason that has determined me to commit to writing these specimens of philosophy is, that I am becoming daily more and more alive to the delay which my design of self-instruction suffers, for want of the infinity of experiments I require, and which it is impossible for me to make without the assistance of others: and, without flattering myself so much as to expect the public to take a large share in my interests, I am yet unwilling to be found so far wanting in the duty I owe to myself, as to give occasion to those who shall survive me to make it matter of reproach against me some day, that I might have left them many things in a much more perfect state than I have done, had I not too much neglected to make them aware of the ways in which they could have promoted the accomplishment of my designs.

And I thought that it was easy for me to select some matters which should neither be obnoxious to much controversy, nor should compel me to expound more of my principles than I desired, and which should yet be sufficient clearly to exhibit what I can or cannot accomplish in the sciences. Whether or not I have succeeded in this it is not for me to say; and I do not wish to forestall the judgments of others by speaking myself of my writings; but it will gratify me if they be examined, and, to afford the greater inducement to this I request all who may have any objections to make to them, to take the trouble of forwarding these to my publisher, who will give me notice of them, that I may endeavor to subjoin at the same time my reply; and in this way readers seeing both at once will more easily determine where the truth lies; for I do not engage in any case to make prolix replies, but only with perfect frankness to avow my errors if I am convinced of them, or if I cannot perceive them, simply to state what I think is required for defense of the matters I have written, adding thereto no explication of any new matte that it may not be necessary to pass without end from one thing to another.

If some of the matters of which I have spoken in the beginning of the "Dioptrics" and "Meteorics" should offend at first sight, because I call them hypotheses and seem indifferent about giving proof of them, I request a patient and attentive reading of the whole, from which I hope those hesitating will derive satisfaction; for it appears to me that the reasonings are so mutually connected in these treatises, that, as the last are demonstrated by the first which are their causes, the first are in their turn demonstrated by the last which are their effects. Nor must it be imagined that I here commit the fallacy which the logicians call a circle; for since experience renders the majority of these effects most certain, the causes from which I deduce them do not serve so much to establish their reality as to explain their existence; but on the contrary, the reality of the causes is established by the reality of the effects. Nor have I called them hypotheses with any other end in view except that it may be known that I think I am able to deduce them from those first truths which I have already expounded; and yet that I have expressly determined not to do so, to prevent a certain class of minds from thence taking occasion to build some extravagant philosophy upon what they may take to be my principles, and my being blamed for it. I refer to those who imagine that they can master in a day all that another has taken twenty years to think out, as soon as he has spoken two or three words to them on the subject; or who are the more liable to error and the less capable of perceiving truth in very proportion as they are more subtle and lively. As to the opinions which are truly and wholly mine, I offer no apology for them as new,—persuaded as I am that if their reasons be well considered they will be found to be so simple and so conformed, to common sense as to appear less extraordinary and less paradoxical than any others which can be held on the same subjects; nor do I even boast of being the earliest discoverer of any of them, but only of having adopted them, neither because they had nor because they had not been held by others, but solely because reason has convinced me of their truth.

Though artisans may not be able at once to execute the invention which is explained in the "Dioptrics," I do not think that any one on that account is entitled to condemn it; for since address and practice are required in order so to make and adjust the machines described by me as not to overlook the smallest particular, I should not be less astonished if they succeeded on the first attempt than if a person were in one day to become an accomplished performer on the guitar, by merely having excellent sheets of music set up before him. And if I write in French, which is the language of my country, in preference to Latin, which is that of my preceptors, it is because I expect that those who make use of their unprejudiced natural reason will be better judges of my opinions than those who give heed to the writings of the ancients only; and as for those who unite good sense with habits of study, whom alone I desire for judges, they will not, I feel assured, be so partial to Latin as to refuse to listen to my reasonings merely because I expound them in the vulgar tongue.

In conclusion, I am unwilling here to say anything very specific of the progress which I expect to make for the future in the sciences, or to bind myself to the public by any promise which I am not certain of being able to fulfill; but this only will I say, that I have resolved to devote what time I may still have to live to no other occupation than that of endeavoring to acquire some knowledge of Nature, which shall be of such a kind as to enable us therefrom to deduce rules in medicine of greater certainty than those at present in use; and that my inclination is so much opposed to all other pursuits, especially to such as cannot be useful to some without being hurtful to others, that if, by any circumstances, I had been constrained to engage in such, I do not believe that I should have been able to succeed. Of this I here make a public declaration, though well aware that it cannot serve to procure for me any consideration in the world, which, however, I do not in the least affect; and I shall always hold myself more obliged to those through whose favor I am permitted to enjoy my retirement without interruption than to any who might offer me the highest earthly preferments.